This Book Belongs to:

_____

_____

_____

_____

If Lost, Please Contact Us:

_____

_____

_____

_____

"There is nothing so American as our national parks,
The fundamental idea behind the parks, is that the countr
belongs to the people, that it is in process of making
for the enrichment of the lives of all of us."

President Franklin D. Roosevе

Tracking Log

№	US National Park	Location	Date Visited
1	Acadia	Maine	
2	American Samoa	American Samoa	
3	Arches	Utah	
4	Badlands	South Dakota	
5	Big Bend	Texas	
6	Biscayne	Florida	
7	Black Canyon of the Gunnison	Colorado	
8	Bryce Canyon	Utah	
9	Canyonlands	Utah	
0	Capitol Reef	Utah	
1	Carlsbad Caverns	New Mexico	
2	Channel Islands	California	
3	Congaree	South Carolina	
4	Crater Lake	Oregon	
5	Cuyahoga Valley	Ohio	
6	Death Valley	California	

Tracking Log

Nº	US National Park	Location	Date Visited
17	Denali	Alaska	
18	Dry Tortugas	Florida	
19	Everglades	Florida	
20	Gates of the Arctic	Alaska	
21	Gateway Arch	Missouri	
22	Glacier Bay	Alaska	
23	Glacier	Montana	
24	Grand Canyon	Arizona	
25	Grand Teton	Wyoming	
26	Great Basin	Nevada	
27	Great Sand Dunes	Colorado	
28	Great Smoky Mountains	North Carolina	
29	Guadalupe Mountains	Texas	
30	Haleakalā	Hawaii	
31	Hawai'i Volcanoes	Hawaii	
32	Hot Springs	Arkansas	

Tracking Log

o	US National Park	Location	Date Visited
3	Indiana Dunes	Indiana	
4	Isle Royale	Michigan	
5	Joshua Tree	California	
6	Katmai	Alaska	
7	Kenai Fjords	Alaska	
8	Kings Canyon	California	
9	Kobuk Valley	Alaska	
0	Lake Clark	Alaska	
1	Lassen Volcanic	California	
2	Mammoth Cave	Kentucky	
3	Mesa Verde	Colorado	
4	Mount Rainier	Washington	
5	New River Gorge	West Virginia	
6	North Cascades	Washington	
7	Olympic	Washington	
8	Petrified Forest	Arizona	

Tracking Log

Nº	US National Park	Location	Date Visited
49	Pinnacles	California	
50	Redwood	California	
51	Rocky Mountain	Colorado	
52	Saguaro	Arizona	
53	Sequoia	California	
54	Shenandoah	Virginia	
55	Theodore Roosevelt	North Dakota	
56	Virgin Islands	Virgin Islands	
57	Voyageurs	Minnesota	
58	White Sands	New Mexico	
59	Wind Cave	South Dakota	
60	Wrangell–St. Elias	Alaska	
61	Yellowstone	Wyoming, Montana & Idaho	
62	Yosemite	California	
63	Zion	Utah	

Acadia

Maine | EST. 1919 | Area (acres): 49076.63 | 44.35N 68.21W

City/State Entered

Dates Visited

Weather

Temp

Where We Stayed

Who Was With Me

What We Did

Sights

Wildlife

Impressions

My Favorite memory

I Visited

- ○ Cadillac Mountain
- ○ Sand Beach
- ○ Jordan Pond
- ○ Park Loop Road
- ○ Carriage Road
- ○ Bass Harbor Lighthouse

- ○ Thunder Hole
- ○ Beehive Trail
- ○ Schoodic Peninsula
- ○ ....
- ○ ....
- ○ ....

Next Time I Will

Notes

Will Return?

Yes / No

Overall Experience

American Samoa

American Samoa | EST. 1988 | Area (acres): 8256.67 | 14.25S 170.68W

City/State Entered

Dates Visited

Weather

Temp

Where We Stayed

Who Was With Me

What We Did

Sights

Wildlife

Impressions

My Favorite Memory

I Visited

- ○ Jean P Haydon Museum
- ○ Mount 'Alava
- ○ Pago Pago Harbour
- ○ Tafeu Cove
- ○ WW2 heritage Trail
- ○ Pola Island
- ○ Blunts Point Trail
- ○ Utulei Beach Park
- ○ Fagatogo Market
- ○ ....
- ○ ....
- ○ ....

Next Time i Will

Notes

Will Return?

Yes / No

Overall Experience

Arches

Utah | EST. 1971 | Area (acres): 76678.98 | 38.68N 109.57W

City/State Entered

Dates Visited

Weather

Temp

Where We Stayed

Who Was With Me

What We Did

Sights

Wildlife

Impressions

My Favorite Memory

I Visited

○ Delicate Arch   ○ Fiery Furnace

○ Landscape Arch   ○ Corona Arch

○ Balanced Rock   ○ Devil's Garden Trailhead

○ Devils Garden   ○ ....

○ Double Arch   ○ ....

○ Slickrock Bike Trail   ○ ....

Next Time I Will

Notes

Will Return?

Yes / No

Overall Experience

Badlands

outh Dakota | EST. 1978 | Area (acres): 242755.94 | 43.75N 102.50W

City/State Entered

Dates Visited

Weather

Temp

Where We Stayed

Who Was With Me

What We Did

Sights

Wildlife

Impressions

My Favorite Memory

I Visited

- ◯ Minuteman Visitors Center
- ◯ Notch Trail
- ◯ Ben Reifel Visitor Center
- ◯ Pinnacles Overlook
- ◯ Yellow Mounds Overlook
- ◯ Roberts Prairie Dog Town
- ◯ The Door Trail
- ◯ Big Badlands Overlook
- ◯ Fossil Exhibit Trailhead
- ◯ ....
- ◯ ....
- ◯ ....

Next Time I Will

Notes

Will Return?

Yes / No

Overall Experience

Big Bend

Texas | EST. 1944 | Area (acres): 801163.21 | 29.25N 103.25W

City/State Entered

Dates Visited

Weather

Temp

Where We Stayed

Who Was With Me

What We Did

Sights

Wildlife

Impressions

My Favorite Memory

I Visited

○ Santa Elena Canyon ○ Boquillas Canyon

○ Emory Peak ○ Maxwell Scenic Drive

○ Lost Mine Trail ○ ....

○ South Rim Trail ○ ....

○ Window Trail ○ ....

○ Grapevine Hills Trail ○ ....

Next Time I Will

Notes

Will Return?

Yes / No

Overall Experience

Biscayne

Florida | EST. 1980 | Area (acres): 172971.11 | 25.65N 80.08W

City/State Entered

Dates Visited

Weather

Temp

Where We Stayed

Who Was With Me

What We Did

Sights

Wildlife

Impressions

My Favorite Memory

I Visited

- ◯ Boca Chita Key ◯ ....
- ◯ Maritime Heritage Trail ◯ ....
- ◯ Dante Fascell Visitor Center ◯ ....
- ◯ Jones Family District ◯ ....
- ◯ Elliott Key ◯ ....
- ◯ Stiltsville ◯ ....

Next Time I Will

Notes

Will Return?

Yes / No

Overall Experience

Black Canyon of the Gunnison

Colorado | EST. 1999 | Area (acres): 30779.83 | 38.57N 107.72W

City/State Entered

Dates Visited

Weather

Temp

Where We Stayed

Who Was With Me

What We Did

Sights

Wildlife

Impressions

My Favorite Memory

I Visited

- ◯ South Rim Road
- ◯ Museum of the Mountain
- ◯ East Portal Road
- ◯ Painted Wall
- ◯ Chasm View Nature Trail
- ◯ South Rim Visitor Center
- ◯ North Vista Trail
- ◯ Gunnison Point
- ◯ Cedar Point Nature Trail
- ◯ ....
- ◯ ....
- ◯ ....

Next Time I Will

Notes

Will Return?

Yes / No

Overall Experience

☆ ☆ ☆ ☆ ☆

Bryce Canyon

Utah | EST. 1928 | Area (acres): 35835.08 | 37.57N 112.18W

City/State Entered

Dates Visited

Weather

Temp

Where We Stayed

Who Was With Me

What We Did

Sights

Wildlife

Impressions

My Favorite Memory

I Visited

- ◯ Sunrise Point
- ◯ Navajo Loop Trail
- ◯ Queens Garden Trail
- ◯ Rim Trail
- ◯ Fairyland Loop Trail
- ◯ Rainbow Point

- ◯ Bryce Amphitheater
- ◯ Bryce Point
- ◯ Yovimpa Point
- ◯ ....
- ◯ ....
- ◯ ....

Next Time I Will

Notes

Will Return?

Yes / No

Overall Experience

Canyonlands

Utah | EST. 1964 | Area (acres): 337597.83 | 38.2N 109.93W

City/State Entered

Dates Visited

Weather

Temp

Where We Stayed

Who Was With Me

What We Did

Sights

Wildlife

Impressions

My Favorite Memory

I Visited

- ◯ Dead Horse Point Park ◯ Chesler Park
- ◯ Island in the Sky Visitor Center ◯ Grand View Point Road
- ◯ Mesa Arch ◯ Green River Overlook
- ◯ Upheaval Dome ◯ ....
- ◯ Needles Visitor Center ◯ ....
- ◯ Needles District ◯ ....

Next Time I Will

Notes

Will Return?

Yes / No

Overall Experience

Capitol Reef

Utah | EST. 1971 | Area (acres): 241904.5 | 38.20N 111.17W

City/State Entered

Dates Visited

Weather

Temp

Where We Stayed

Who Was With Me

What We Did

Sights

Wildlife

Impressions

My Favorite Memory

I Visited

- ◯ Water Pocket Fold
- ◯ Capitol Reef
- ◯ Cassidy Arch
- ◯ Fremont river
- ◯ Hickman Bridge Trail
- ◯ Cathedral Valley Road
- ◯ Hickman Natural Bridge
- ◯ Grand Washington
- ◯ Strike Valley Overlook
- ◯ ....
- ◯ ....
- ◯ ....

Next Time I Will

Notes

Will Return?

Yes / No

Overall Experience

☆ ☆ ☆ ☆ ☆

Carlsbad Caverns

New Mexico | EST. 1930 | Area (acres): 46766.45 | 32.17N 104.44W

City/State Entered

Dates Visited

Weather

Temp

Where We Stayed

Who Was With Me

What We Did

Sights

Wildlife

Impressions

My Favorite Memory

I Visited

- ◯ Cavern Natural Entrance ◯ ....
- ◯ National Park Visitor ◯ ....
- ◯ Slaughter Canyon Cave ◯ ....
- ◯ Caverns Wilderness ◯ ....
- ◯ Lechuguilla Canyon ◯ ....
- ◯ .... ◯ ....

Next Time I Will

Notes

Will Return?

Yes / No

Overall Experience

Channel Islands

California | EST. 1980 | Area (acres): 249561 | 34.01N 119.42W

City/State Entered

Dates Visited

Weather

Temp

Where We Stayed

Who Was With Me

What We Did

Sights

Wildlife

Impressions

My Favorite Memory

I Visited

- ◯ Anacapa Island
- ◯ Santa Barbara Island
- ◯ Robert Lagomarsino Visitor
- ◯ Painted Cave
- ◯ Channel Islands Marine
- ◯ Marina Park

- ◯ East Anacapa Island
- ◯ Cavern Point
- ◯ Scorpion Anchorage
- ◯ ....
- ◯ ....
- ◯ ....

Next Time I Will

Notes

Will Return?

Yes / No

Overall Experience

☆ ☆ ☆ ☆ ☆

Congaree

South Carolina | EST. 2003 | Area (acres): 26476.47 | 33.78N 80.78W

City/State Entered

Dates Visited

Weather

Temp

Where We Stayed

Who Was With Me

What We Did

Sights

Wildlife

Impressions

My Favorite Memory

I Visited

- ◯ Poinsett State Park
- ◯ Cedar Creek Canoe Launch
- ◯ Weston Lake
- ◯ Congaree Bluffs Preserve
- ◯ Bates Bridge Landing
- ◯ Millford Plantation Site

- ◯ Fork Swamp
- ◯ ....
- ◯ ....
- ◯ ....
- ◯ ....
- ◯ ....

Next Time I Will

Notes

Will Return?

Yes / No

Overall Experience

Crater Lake

Oregon | EST. 1902 | Area (acres): 183224.05 | 42.94N 122.1W

City/State Entered

Dates Visited

Weather

Temp

Where We Stayed

Who Was With Me

What We Did

Sights

Wildlife

Impressions

My Favorite Memory

I visited

- ⃝ Wizard Island
- ⃝ Rim Drive
- ⃝ Mount Mazama
- ⃝ Mount Scott
- ⃝ Phantom Ship
- ⃝ Mount Thielsen

- ⃝ Cleetwood Cove Trail
- ⃝ Garfield Peak
- ⃝ Rim Village District
- ⃝ ....
- ⃝ ....
- ⃝ ....

Next Time I Will

Notes

Will Return?

Yes / No

Overall Experience

Cuyahoga Valley

Ohio | EST. 2000 | Area (acres): 32571.88 | 41.24N 81.55W

City/State Entered

Dates Visited

Weather

Temp

Where We Stayed

Who Was With Me

What We Did

Sights

Wildlife

Impressions

My Favorite Memory

I Visited

- ◯ Scenic Railroad
- ◯ Brandywine Falls
- ◯ Boston Mills Ski Areas
- ◯ Ohio/Erie Canal Towpath Trail
- ◯ Hale Farm & Village
- ◯ Blue Hen Falls

- ◯ Brecksville Reservation
- ◯ Bedford Reservation
- ◯ ....
- ◯ ....
- ◯ ....
- ◯ ....

Next Time I Will

Notes

Will Return?

Yes / No

Overall Experience

☆ ☆ ☆ ☆ ☆

Death Valley

California | EST. 1994 | Area (acres): 3408406.73 | 36.24N 116.82W

City/State Entered

Dates Visited

Weather

Temp

Where We Stayed

Who Was With Me

What We Did

Sights

Wildlife

Impressions

My Favorite Memory

I Visited

- ◯ Zabriskie Point
- ◯ Badwater Basin
- ◯ Dante's View
- ◯ Telescope Peak
- ◯ Ubehebe Crater
- ◯ Racetrack Playa

- ◯ Devils Golf Course
- ◯ Scotty's Castle
- ◯ Mesquite Flat Dunes
- ◯ ....
- ◯ ....
- ◯ ....

Next Time I Will

Notes

Will Return?

Yes / No

Overall Experience

☆ ☆ ☆ ☆ ☆

Denali

Alaska | EST. 1917 | Area (acres): 4740911.16 | 63.33N 150.50W

City/State Entered

Dates Visited

Weather

Temp

Where We Stayed

Who Was With Me

What We Did

Sights

Wildlife

Impressions

My Favorite Memory

I Visited

- ○ Denali
- ○ Wonder Lake
- ○ Denali State Park
- ○ Mount Foraker
- ○ Denali Park Road
- ○ Eielson Visitor Center

- ○ Polychrome Pass
- ○ Stampede Trail
- ○ Mount Hunter
- ○ ....
- ○ ....
- ○ ....

Next Time I Will

Notes

Will Return?

Yes / No

Overall Experience

Dry Tortugas

Florida | EST. 1992 | Area (acres): 64701.22 | 24.63N 82.87W

City/State Entered

Dates Visited

Weather

Temp

Where We Stayed

Who Was With Me

What We Did

Sights

Wildlife

Impressions

My Favorite Memory

I Visited

○ Dry Tortugas
○ Garden Key
○ Loggerhead Key
○ Loggerhead Lighthouse
○ Bush Key
○ Garden Key Lighthouse

○ Pulaski Shoal
○ Hospital Key
○ ....
○ ....
○ ....
○ ....

Next Time I Will

Notes

Will Return?

Yes / No

Overall Experience

Everglades

Florida | EST. 1934 | Area (acres): 1508938.57 | 25.32N 80.93W

City/State Entered

Dates Visited

Weather

Temp

Where We Stayed

Who Was With Me

What We Did

Sights

Wildlife

Impressions

My Favorite Memory

I Visited

- ○ John Pennekamp Park
- ○ Theater of the Sea
- ○ Alligator Farm
- ○ Anhinga Trail
- ○ Robbie's
- ○ Long Key State Park

- ○ Indian Key Park
- ○ Anne's Beach
- ○ ....
- ○ ....
- ○ ....
- ○ ....

Next Time I Will

Notes

Will Return?

Yes / No

Overall Experience

☆ ☆ ☆ ☆ ☆

Gates of the Arctic

Alaska | EST. 1980 | Area (acres): 7523897.45 | 67.78N 153.30W

City/State Entered

Dates Visited

Weather

Temp

Where We Stayed

Who Was With Me

What We Did

Sights

Wildlife

Impressions

My Favorite Memory

I Visited

- ○ Arrigetch Peaks
- ○ Alatna Wild River
- ○ Frigid Crags
- ○ Tinayguk River
- ○ Takahula Lake
- ○ Gates of the Arctic Wilderness

- ○ Mount Igikpak
- ○ Walker Lake
- ○ Endicott Mountains
- ○ ....
- ○ ....
- ○ ....

Next Time I Will

Notes

Will Return?

Yes / No

Overall Experience

☆ ☆ ☆ ☆ ☆

Gateway Arch

Missouri | EST. 2018 | Area (acres): 192.83 | 38.63N 90.19W

City/State Entered

Dates Visited

Weather

Temp

Where We Stayed

Who Was With Me

What We Did

Sights

Wildlife

Impressions

My Favorite Memory

I Visited

○ The Gateway Arch   ○ Laclede's Neighborhood

○ City Museum   ○ St. Louis Aquarium

○ Old Courthouse   ○ Eads Bridge

○ Busch Stadium   ○ ....

○ Citygarden Sculpture Park   ○ ....

○ Blues Museum   ○ ....

Next Time I Will

Notes

Will Return?

Yes / No

Overall Experience

Glacier Bay

Alaska | EST. 1980 | Area (acres): 3223383.43 | 48.80N 114.00W

City/State Entered

Dates Visited

Weather

Temp

Where We Stayed

Who Was With Me

What We Did

Sights

Wildlife

Impressions

My Favorite Memory

I Visited

- ◯ Margerie Glacier
- ◯ Mount Fairweather
- ◯ Lituya Bay
- ◯ Johns Hopkins Glacier
- ◯ Bartlet Cove AK
- ◯ Lamplugh Glacier
- ◯ Lituya Glacier
- ◯ Reid Glacier
- ◯ Muir Glacier
- ◯ ....
- ◯ ....
- ◯ ....

Next Time I Will

Notes

Will Return?

Yes / No

Overall Experience

☆ ☆ ☆ ☆ ☆

Glacier

Montana | EST. 1910 | Area (acres): 1013125.99 | 58.50N 137.00W

City/State Entered

Dates Visited

Weather

Temp

Where We Stayed

Who Was With Me

What We Did

Sights

Wildlife

Impressions

My Favorite Memory

I Visited

- ○ Going-to-the-Sun Road
- ○ Lake McDonald
- ○ Logan Pass
- ○ Saint Mary Lake
- ○ Grinnell Glacier
- ○ Avalanche Lake
- ○ Iceberg Lake
- ○ Swiftcurrent Lake
- ○ Highline Trail
- ○ ....
- ○ ....
- ○ ....

Next Time I Will

Notes

Will Return?

Yes / No

Overall Experience

Grand Canyon

Arizona | EST. 1919 | Area (acres): 1201647.03 | 36.06N 112.14W

City/State Entered

Dates Visited

Weather

Temp

Where We Stayed

Who Was With Me

What We Did

Sights

Wildlife

Impressions

My Favorite Memory

I Visited

- ◯ Grand Canyon Village
- ◯ Bright Angel Trail
- ◯ Havasu Falls
- ◯ Grand Canyon Railway
- ◯ Rim Trail
- ◯ Canyon Visitor Center
- ◯ West Rim Trail
- ◯ Desert Watchtower
- ◯ South Kaibab Trail
- ◯ ....
- ◯ ....
- ◯ ....

Next Time I Will

Notes

Will Return?

Yes / No

Overall Experience

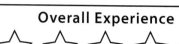

Grand Teton

Wyoming | EST. 1929 | Area (acres): 310044.36 | 43.73N 110.80W

City/State Entered

Dates Visited

Weather

Temp

Where We Stayed

Who Was With Me

What We Did

Sights

Wildlife

Impressions

My Favorite Memory

I Visited

- ◯ Grand Teton
- ◯ Jackson Hole
- ◯ Jenny Lake
- ◯ Jackson Hole Resort
- ◯ Jackson Lake
- ◯ Grand Targhee Resort

- ◯ Jackson Lake Lodge
- ◯ Signal Mountain
- ◯ National Elk Refuge
- ◯ ....
- ◯ ....
- ◯ ....

Next Time I Will

Notes

Will Return?

Yes / No

Overall Experience

☆ ☆ ☆ ☆ ☆

Great Basin

Nevada | EST. 1986 | Area (acres): 77180 | 38.98N 114.30W

City/State Entered

Dates Visited

Weather

Temp

Where We Stayed

Who Was With Me

What We Did

Sights

Wildlife

Impressions

My Favorite Memory

I Visited

- ○ Wheeler Peak
- ○ Lehman Caves
- ○ Forest Development Road
- ○ Stella Lake
- ○ Teresa Lake
- ○ Rock Glacier
- ○ Lehman Caves Visitor Center
- ○ Jeff Davis Peak
- ○ Baker Peak
- ○ ....
- ○ ....
- ○ ....

Next Time I Will

Notes

Will Return?

Yes / No

Overall Experience

☆ ☆ ☆ ☆ ☆

Great Sand Dunes

Colorado | EST. 2004 | Area (acres): 107341.87 | 37.73N 105.51W

City/State Entered

Dates Visited

Weather

Temp

Where We Stayed

Who Was With Me

What We Did

Sights

Wildlife

Impressions

My Favorite Memory

I Visited

- ○ Zapata Falls
- ○ High Dune
- ○ Zapata Ranch
- ○ Medano Pass
- ○ San Luis State Wildlife Area
- ○ Mosca Pass Trail

- ○ San Luis Lake
- ○ Mount Herard
- ○ Medano Creek
- ○ ....
- ○ ....
- ○ ....

Next Time I Will

Notes

Will Return?

Yes / No

Overall Experience

Great Smoky Mountains

North Carolina | EST. 1934 | Area (acres): 522426.88 | 35.68N 83.53W

City/State Entered

Dates Visited

Weather

Temp

Where We Stayed

Who Was With Me

What We Did

Sights

Wildlife

Impressions

My Favorite Memory

I Visited

- ○ Cades Cove
- ○ Clingmans Dome
- ○ Ober Gatlinburg
- ○ Ripley's Aquarium
- ○ Newfound Gap
- ○ Mount Le Conte
- ○ Great Smoky Railroad
- ○ Gatlinburg SkyLift Park
- ○ Oconaluftee Visitor Center
- ○ ....
- ○ ....
- ○ ....

Next Time I Will

Notes

Will Return?

Yes / No

Overall Experience

Guadalupe Mountains

Texas | EST. 1966 | Area (acres): 86367.1 | 31.92N 104.87W

City/State Entered

Dates Visited

Weather

Temp

Where We Stayed

Who Was With Me

What We Did

Sights

Wildlife

Impressions

My Favorite Memory

I Visited

- ◯ Guadalupe Peak
- ◯ Mckittrick Canyon
- ◯ El Capitan
- ◯ Devil's Hall Trail
- ◯ Salt Basin Dunes
- ◯ Frijole Ranch Museum

- ◯ Smith Spring Trail
- ◯ Visitor Center
- ◯ Bush Mountain
- ◯ ....
- ◯ ....
- ◯ ....

Next Time I Will

Notes

Will Return?

Yes / No

Overall Experience

Haleakalā

Hawaii | EST. 1961 | Area (acres): 33264.62 | 20.72N 156.17W

City/State Entered

Dates Visited

Weather

Temp

Where We Stayed

Who Was With Me

What We Did

Sights

Wildlife

Impressions

My Favorite Memory

I Visited

○ Hana Highway   ○ Haleakalā Park Entrance

○ The Pools at 'Ohe'o   ○ Keonehe'ehe'e Trail

○ Pipiwai Trail   ○ Pīpīwai Trail

○ Waimoku Falls   ○ ....

○ 'Ohe'o Gulch   ○ ....

○ Haleakalā Crater   ○ ....

Next Time I Will

Notes

Will Return?

Yes / No

Overall Experience

Hawai'i Volcanoes

Hawaii | EST. 1916 | Area (acres): 325605.28 | 19.38N 155.20W

City/State Entered

Dates Visited

Weather

Temp

Where We Stayed

Who Was With Me

What We Did

Sights

Wildlife

Impressions

My Favorite Memory

I Visited

- ○ Kīlauea
- ○ Nāhuku - Thurston Lava Tube
- ○ Chain of Craters Road
- ○ Halemaumau Crater
- ○ Kīlauea Iki Crater
- ○ Pu'u 'Ō'ō
- ○ Crater Rim Drive
- ○ Visitor Center
- ○ Kilauea Iki Trail
- ○ ....
- ○ ....
- ○ ....

Next Time I Will

Notes

Will Return?

Yes / No

Overall Experience

Hot Springs

Arkansas | EST. 1921 | Area (acres): 5554.15 | 34.51N 93.05W

City/State Entered	Dates Visited

Weather

Temp

Where We Stayed

Who Was With Me

What We Did

Sights

Wildlife

Impressions

My Favorite Memory

I Visited

- ○ Hot Springs Tower
- ○ Magic Springs
- ○ Gangster Museum
- ○ Fordyce Bathhouse
- ○ Oaklawn Racing
- ○ Arkansas Alligator Farm

- ○ Tussaud Wax Museum
- ○ America Science Museum
- ○ The Grand Promenade
- ○ ....
- ○ ....
- ○ ....

Next Time I Will

Notes

Will Return?

Yes / No

Overall Experience

Indiana Dunes

Indiana | EST. 2019 | Area (acres): 15349.08 | 41.6533N 87.0524W

City/State Entered

Dates Visited

Weather

Temp

Where We Stayed

Who Was With Me

What We Did

Sights

Wildlife

Impressions

My Favorite Memory

I Visited

- ◯ Indiana Dunes Park
- ◯ Deep River Waterpark
- ◯ Old Lighthouse Museum
- ◯ Mount Baldy
- ◯ Barker Mansion
- ◯ Majestic Star Casino
- ◯ Visitor Center
- ◯ Access to West Beach
- ◯ Friendship Botanic Gardens
- ◯ ....
- ◯ ....
- ◯ ....

Next Time I Will

Notes

Will Return?

Yes / No

Overall Experience

Isle Royale

Michigan | EST. 1940 | Area (acres): 571790.3 | 48.10N 88.55W

City/State Entered

Dates Visited

Weather

Temp

Where We Stayed

Who Was With Me

What We Did

Sights

Wildlife

Impressions

My Favorite Memory

I Visited

- ◯ Rock Harbor
- ◯ Minong Ridge
- ◯ Windigo
- ◯ Lookout Louise
- ◯ Rock Harbor Lighthouse
- ◯ Scoville Point

- ◯ Rock of Ages Lighthouse
- ◯ Feldtmann Lake
- ◯ Lake Desor
- ◯ ....
- ◯ ....
- ◯ ....

Next Time I Will

Notes

Will Return?

Yes / No

Overall Experience

Joshua Tree

California | EST. 1994 | Area (acres): 795155.85 | 33.79N 115.90W

City/State Entered

Dates Visited

Weather

Temp

Where We Stayed

Who Was With Me

What We Did

Sights

Wildlife

Impressions

My Favorite Memory

I Visited

- ◯ Keys View
- ◯ Skull Rock
- ◯ Barker Dam
- ◯ Coachella Valley Preserve
- ◯ Cholla Cactus Garden
- ◯ Hidden Valley Nature Trail

- ◯ Lost Palms Oasis Trail
- ◯ Arch Rock
- ◯ Ryan Mountain
- ◯ ....
- ◯ ....
- ◯ ....

Next Time I Will

Notes

Will Return?

Yes / No

Overall Experience

☆ ☆ ☆ ☆ ☆

Katmai

Alaska | EST. 1980 | Area (acres): 3674529.33 | 58.50N 155.00W

City/State Entered

Dates Visited

Weather

Temp

Where We Stayed

Who Was With Me

What We Did

Sights

Wildlife

Impressions

My Favorite Memory

I Visited

○ Brooks Falls
○ Mount Katmai
○ Valley of 10K Smokes
○ Brooks River
○ Hallo Bay
○ Novarupta

○ Markland
○ American Creek
○ Moraine Creek
○ ....
○ ....
○ ....

Next Time I Will

Notes

Will Return?

Yes / No

Overall Experience

Kenai Fjords

Alaska | EST. 1980 | Area (acres): 669650.05 | 59.92N 149.65W

City/State Entered

Dates Visited

Weather

Temp

Where We Stayed

Who Was With Me

What We Did

Sights

Wildlife

Impressions

My Favorite Memory

I Visited

- ○ Exit Glacier
- ○ Bear Glacier
- ○ Aialik Glacier
- ○ Kachemak Bay Park
- ○ Aialik Bay
- ○ Holgate Glacier
- ○ Grewingk Glacier
- ○ Tonsina Point
- ○ Pedersen Glacier
- ○ ....
- ○ ....
- ○ ....

Next Time I Will

Notes

Will Return?

Yes / No

Overall Experience

☆ ☆ ☆ ☆ ☆

Kings Canyon

California | EST. 1940 | Area (acres): 461901.2 | 36.80N 118.55W

City/State Entered

Dates Visited

Weather

Temp

Where We Stayed

Who Was With Me

What We Did

Sights

Wildlife

Impressions

My Favorite Memory

I Visited

- ◯ General Grant Grove
- ◯ Hume Lake
- ◯ John Muir Wilderness
- ◯ Generals Highway
- ◯ Rae Lakes Loop Trailhead
- ◯ Zumwalt Meadows
- ◯ John Muir Trail
- ◯ Lake Sabrina
- ◯ Rae Lakes
- ◯ ....
- ◯ ....
- ◯ ....

Next Time I Will

Notes

Will Return?

Yes / No

Overall Experience

Kobuk Valley

Alaska | EST. 1980 | Area (acres): 1750716.16 | 67.55N 159.28W

City/State Entered

Dates Visited

Weather

Temp

Where We Stayed

Who Was With Me

What We Did

Sights

Wildlife

Impressions

My Favorite Memory

I Visited

- ○ Great Kobuk Sand Dunes
- ○ Hunt River
- ○ Jade Mountains
- ○ ....
- ○ ....
- ○ ....

- ○ ....
- ○ ....
- ○ ....
- ○ ....
- ○ ....
- ○ ....

Next Time I Will

Notes

Will Return?

Yes / No

Overall Experience

Lake Clark

Alaska | EST. 1980 | Area (acres): 2619816.49 | 60.97N 153.42W

City/State Entered

Dates Visited

Weather

Temp

Where We Stayed

Who Was With Me

What We Did

Sights

Wildlife

Impressions

My Favorite Memory

I Visited

- ◯ Turquoise Lake
- ◯ Telaquana Lake
- ◯ Chilikadrotna River
- ◯ Tlikakila River
- ◯ Kontrashibuna Lake
- ◯ Tanalian Falls Trailhead
- ◯ Tanalian Mountain
- ◯ Kijik District
- ◯ Snipe Lake
- ◯ ....
- ◯ ....
- ◯ ....

Next Time I Will

Notes

Will Return?

Yes / No

Overall Experience

☆ ☆ ☆ ☆ ☆

Lassen Volcanic

California | EST. 1916 | Area (acres): 106589.02 | 40.49N 121.51W

City/State Entered

Dates Visited

Weather

Temp

Where We Stayed

Who Was With Me

What We Did

Sights

Wildlife

Impressions

My Favorite Memory

I Visited

- ○ Lassen Peak
- ○ Manzanita Lake
- ○ Lassen Forest
- ○ Cinder Cone
- ○ Lake Helen
- ○ Mount Tehama

- ○ Bumpass Hell
- ○ Butte Lake
- ○ Kings Creek Falls
- ○ ....
- ○ ....
- ○ ....

Next Time I Will

Notes

Will Return?

Yes / No

Overall Experience

Mammoth Cave

Kentucky | EST. 1941 | Area (acres): 54011.91 | 37.18N 86.10W

City/State Entered

Dates Visited

Weather

Temp

Where We Stayed

Who Was With Me

What We Did

Sights

Wildlife

Impressions

My Favorite Memory

I Visited

- ◯ Diamond Caverns
- ◯ Dinosaur World
- ◯ Guntown Mountain
- ◯ Nolin River Lake
- ◯ Nolin Lake
- ◯ Wildlife Museum

- ◯ CRYSTAL ONYX Cave
- ◯ Historic Entrance
- ◯ Gothic Avenue Tour
- ◯ ....
- ◯ ....
- ◯ ....

Next Time I Will

Notes

Will Return?

Yes / No

Overall Experience

Mesa Verde

Colorado | EST. 1906 | Area (acres): 52485.17 | 37.18N 108.49W

City/State Entered

Dates Visited

Weather

Temp

Where We Stayed

Who Was With Me

What We Did

Sights

Wildlife

Impressions

My Favorite Memory

I Visited

- ○ Cliff Palace
- ○ Balcony House
- ○ Spruce Tree House
- ○ Mesa Top Loop
- ○ Square Tower House
- ○ Long House

- ○ Visitor and Research Center
- ○ Spruce Canyon Trail
- ○ Wetherill Mesa
- ○ ....
- ○ ....
- ○ ....

Next Time I Will

Notes

Will Return?

Yes / No

Overall Experience

☆ ☆ ☆ ☆ ☆

Mount Rainier

Washington | EST. 1899 | Area (acres): 236381.64 | 46.85N 121.75W

City/State Entered

Dates Visited

Weather

Temp

Where We Stayed

Who Was With Me

What We Did

Sights

Wildlife

Impressions

My Favorite Memory

I Visited

- ◯ Mount Rainier
- ◯ Crystal Mountain
- ◯ Narada Falls
- ◯ Tipsoo Lake
- ◯ Henry Jackson Center
- ◯ Gifford Pinchot Forest

- ◯ Mowich Lake
- ◯ Christine Falls
- ◯ Chinook Pass
- ◯ ....
- ◯ ....
- ◯ ....

Next Time I Will

Notes

Will Return?

Yes / No

Overall Experience

New River Gorge

West Virginia | EST. 2020 | Area (acres): 7021 | 38.07N 81.08W

City/State Entered

Dates Visited

Weather

Temp

Where We Stayed

Who Was With Me

What We Did

Sights

Wildlife

Impressions

My Favorite Memory

I Visited

- ○ Babcock State Park
- ○ Bank of Glen Jean
- ○ Canyon Rim
- ○ Fayette Station
- ○ Kaymoor
- ○ Hawks Nest Park
- ○ Nuttallburg Complex
- ○ Prince
- ○ Sandstone Falls
- ○ Thurmond Depot
- ○ ....
- ○ ....

Next Time I Will

Notes

Will Return?

Yes / No

Overall Experience

☆ ☆ ☆ ☆ ☆

North Cascades

Washington | EST. 1968 | Area (acres): 504780.94 | 48.70N 121.20W

City/State Entered

Dates Visited

Weather

Temp

Where We Stayed

Who Was With Me

What We Did

Sights

Wildlife

Impressions

My Favorite Memory

I Visited

- ○ Diablo Lake
- ○ Mt. Baker Ski Area
- ○ Ross Lake
- ○ Mount Shuksan
- ○ Cascade Pass
- ○ Ross Lake Recreation Area

- ○ Baker Lake
- ○ Washington Pass
- ○ Maple Pass
- ○ ....
- ○ ....
- ○ ....

Next Time I Will

Notes

Will Return?

Yes / No

Overall Experience

☆ ☆ ☆ ☆ ☆

Olympic

Washington | EST. 1938 | Area (acres): 922649.41 | 47.97N 123.50W

City/State Entered

Dates Visited

Weather

Temp

Where We Stayed

Who Was With Me

What We Did

Sights

Wildlife

Impressions

My Favorite Memory

I visited

- ◯ Hoh Rain Visitor Center
- ◯ Hurricane Ridge
- ◯ Lake Crescent
- ◯ Sol Duc River
- ◯ Ruby Beach
- ◯ Marymere Falls
- ◯ Lake Quinault
- ◯ Olympic National Forest
- ◯ Mount Olympus
- ◯ ....
- ◯ ....
- ◯ ....

Next Time I Will

Notes

Will Return?

Yes / No

Overall Experience

Petrified Forest

Arizona | EST. 1962 | Area (acres): 221390.21 | 35.07N 109.78W

City/State Entered

Dates Visited

Weather

Temp

Where We Stayed

Who Was With Me

What We Did

Sights

Wildlife

Impressions

My Favorite Memory

I Visited

- ◯ Blue Mesa
- ◯ Painted Desert Inn
- ◯ Crystal Forest
- ◯ Agate House Pueblo
- ◯ Jasper Forest
- ◯ Rainbow Forest

- ◯ Newspaper Rock
- ◯ Rainbow Forest Museum
- ◯ Puerco Pueblo
- ◯ ....
- ◯ ....
- ◯ ....

Next Time I Will

Notes

Will Return?

Yes / No

Overall Experience

☆ ☆ ☆ ☆ ☆

Pinnacles

California | EST. 2013 | Area (acres): 26685.73 | 36.48N 121.16W

City/State Entered

Dates Visited

Weather

Temp

Where We Stayed

Who Was With Me

What We Did

Sights

Wildlife

Impressions

My Favorite Memory

I Visited

- ○ Bear Gulch Cave Trail
- ○ High Peaks Trail
- ○ Balconies Cave Trail
- ○ Condor Gulch Trail
- ○ Bear Gulch Reservoir
- ○ Bear Gulch Day Use Area
- ○ High Peaks
- ○ Chalone Peak Trail
- ○ North Chalone Peak
- ○ ....
- ○ ....
- ○ ....

Next Time I Will

Notes

Will Return?

Yes / No

Overall Experience

Redwood

California | EST. 1968 | Area (acres): 138999.37 | 41.30N 124.00W

City/State Entered

Dates Visited

Weather

Temp

Where We Stayed

Who Was With Me

What We Did

Sights

Wildlife

Impressions

My favorite memory

I Visited

- ◯ Jedediah Smith State Park ◯ Trees of Mystery
- ◯ Redwood State Park ◯ Gold Bluffs Beach
- ◯ Prairie Creek State Park ◯ Lady Bird Johnson Trail
- ◯ Fern Canyon ◯ ....
- ◯ Prairie Creek ◯ ....
- ◯ Del Norte Coast Park ◯ ....

Next Time I Will

Notes

Will Return?

Yes / No

Overall Experience

Rocky Mountain

Colorado | EST. 1915 | Area (acres): 265807.25 | 40.40N 105.58W

City/State Entered

Dates Visited

Weather

Temp

Where We Stayed

Who Was With Me

What We Did

Sights

Wildlife

Impressions

My Favorite Memory

I Visited

- ⭕ Trail Ridge Road
- ⭕ Longs Peak
- ⭕ Bear Lake
- ⭕ Dream Lake
- ⭕ Alpine Visitor Center
- ⭕ Emerald Lake
- ⭕ Sprague Lake
- ⭕ Beaver Visitor Center
- ⭕ Old Fall River Road
- ⭕ ....
- ⭕ ....
- ⭕ ....

Next Time I Will

Notes

Will Return?

Yes / No

Overall Experience

☆ ☆ ☆ ☆ ☆

Saguaro

Arizona | EST. 1994 | Area (acres): 92867.42 | 32.25N 110.50W

City/State Entered

Dates Visited

Weather

☀ ⛅ ☁ ⛈ 🌬 ❄

Temp

Where We Stayed

Who Was With Me

What We Did

Sights

Wildlife

Impressions

My Favorite Memory

I Visited

- ○ Sonora Desert Museum
- ○ Tucson Mountain Park
- ○ Old Tucson
- ○ Agua Caliente Park
- ○ Rincon Mountains
- ○ Douglas Spring Trailhead
- ○ Wildlife Museum
- ○ ....
- ○ Gates Pass
- ○ ....
- ○ Rincon Visitor Center
- ○ ....

Next Time I Will

Notes

Will Return?

Yes / No

Overall Experience

Sequoia

California | EST. 1890 | Area (acres): 404062.63 | 36.43N 118.68W

City/State Entered

Dates Visited

Weather

Temp

Where We Stayed

Who Was With Me

What We Did

Sights

Wildlife

Impressions

My Favorite Memory

I Visited

- ◯ General Sherman Tree
- ◯ Mount Whitney
- ◯ Sequoia & Kings
- ◯ Giant Forest
- ◯ Crystal Cave
- ◯ Sequoia Tunnel Log
- ◯ Crescent Meadow Road
- ◯ High Sierra Trailhead
- ◯ ....
- ◯ ....
- ◯ ....
- ◯ ....

Next Time I Will

Notes

Will Return?

Yes / No

Overall Experience

Shenandoah

Virginia | EST. 1935 | Area (acres): 199223.77 | 38.53N 78.35W

City/State Entered

Dates Visited

Weather

Temp

Where We Stayed

Who Was With Me

What We Did

Sights

Wildlife

Impressions

My Favorite Memory

I Visited

- ○ Skyline Drive
- ○ Luray Caverns
- ○ Old Rag Mountain
- ○ Massanutten Resort
- ○ Hawksbill Mountain
- ○ Whiteoak Canyon Trail

- ○ Stony Man
- ○ Dark Hollow Falls
- ○ Mary's Rock
- ○ ....
- ○ ....
- ○ ....

Next Time I Will

Notes

Will Return?

Yes / No

Overall Experience

Theodore Roosevelt

North Dakota | EST. 1978 | Area (acres): 70446.89 | 46.97N 103.45W

City/State Entered

Dates Visited

Weather

Temp

Where We Stayed

Who Was With Me

What We Did

Sights

Wildlife

Impressions

My Favorite Memory

I Visited

○ Maah Daah Hey Trail ○ Maltese Cross Cabin

○ Chateau de Mores ○ Elkhorn Ranch

○ South Unit Visitor Center ○ Wind Canyon Trail

○ ND Cowboy Hall of Fame ○ ....

○ Bully Pulpit Golf Course ○ ....

○ Sully Creek State Park ○ ....

Next Time I Will

Notes

Will Return?

Yes / No

Overall Experience

Virgin Islands

Virgin Islands | EST. 1956 | Area (acres): 15052.53 | 18.33N 64.73W

City/State Entered

Dates Visited

Weather

Temp

Where We Stayed

Who Was With Me

What We Did

Sights

Wildlife

Impressions

My Favorite Memory

I Visited

- ○ Trunk Bay
- ○ Cinnamon Bay
- ○ Blackbeard's Castle
- ○ Waterlemon Cay
- ○ Honeymoon Beach
- ○ 99 Steps

- ○ Fort Christian
- ○ Reef Bay Trail
- ○ ....
- ○ ....
- ○ ....
- ○ ....

Next Time I Will

Notes

Will Return?

Yes / No

Overall Experience

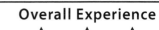

Voyageurs

Minnesota | EST. 1975 | Area (acres): 218222.35 | 48.50N 92.88W

City/State Entered

Dates Visited

Weather

Temp

Where We Stayed

Who Was With Me

What We Did

Sights

Wildlife

Impressions

My Favorite Memory

I Visited

○ Ash River Visitor Center   ○ Namakan Lake

○ Northern Lights Resort   ○ Sand Point Lake

○ Ellsworth Rock Gardens   ○ Cruiser Lake Trail

○ Rainy Lake Visitor Center   ○ ....

○ Grassy Bay Cliffs   ○ ....

○ Echo Bay Trail   ○ ....

Next Time I Will

Notes

Will Return?

Yes / No

Overall Experience

White Sands

New Mexico | EST. 2019 | Area (acres): 146344.31 | 32.78N 106.17W

City/State Entered

Dates Visited

Weather

Temp

Where We Stayed

Who Was With Me

What We Did

Sights

Wildlife

Impressions

My Favorite Memory

I Visited

- ○ Lake Lucero
- ○ Dunes Life Nature Trail
- ○ Interdune Boardwalk
- ○ Playa Trail
- ○ White Sands Visitor Center
- ○ Sunset Stroll Meeting Area
- ○ White Sands Historic District
- ○ ....
- ○ ....
- ○ ....
- ○ ....
- ○ ....

Next Time I Will

Notes

Will Return?

Yes / No

Overall Experience

Wind Cave

South Dakota | EST. 1903 | Area (acres): 33970.84 | 43.57N 103.48W

City/State Entered

Dates Visited

Weather

Temp

Where We Stayed

Who Was With Me

What We Did

Sights

Wildlife

Impressions

My Favorite Memory

I Visited

- ◯ Visitor Center
- ◯ Rankin Ridge
- ◯ Wind Cave Canyon
- ◯ Rankin Ridge Trail
- ◯ Lookout Point Trail
- ◯ Centennial Trail #89

- ◯ Cold Brook Canyon Trail
- ◯ Boland Ridge
- ◯ Elk Mountain
- ◯ ....
- ◯ ....
- ◯ ....

Next Time I Will

Notes

Will Return?

Yes / No

Overall Experience

Wrangell St. Elias

Alaska | EST. 1980 | Area (acres): 8323146.48 | 61.00N 142.00W

City/State Entered

Dates Visited

Weather

Temp

Where We Stayed

Who Was With Me

What We Did

Sights

Wildlife

Impressions

My Favorite Memory

I Visited

- ◯ Hubbard Glacier
- ◯ Mount Wrangell
- ◯ Mount Blackburn
- ◯ Mount Sanford
- ◯ Kennicott Glacier
- ◯ Mount Bona

- ◯ Root Glacier
- ◯ Nizina River
- ◯ Root Glacier Trail
- ◯ ....
- ◯ ....
- ◯ ....

Next Time I Will

Notes

Will Return?

Yes / No

Overall Experience

Yellowstone

WY, MT, ID | EST. 1872 | Area (acres): 2219790.71 | 44.60N 110.50W

City/State Entered

Dates Visited

Weather

Temp

Where We Stayed

Who Was With Me

What We Did

Sights

Wildlife

Impressions

My Favorite Memory

I Visited

- ◯ Old Faithful
- ◯ Grand Prismatic Spring
- ◯ Yellowstone Lake
- ◯ Yellowstone Caldera
- ◯ Upper Falls of the River
- ◯ Mammoth Hot Springs
- ◯ Old Faithful Inn
- ◯ Morning Glory Pool
- ◯ ....
- ◯ ....
- ◯ ....
- ◯ ....

Next Time I Will

Notes

Will Return?

Yes / No

Overall Experience

Yosemite

California | EST. 1890 | Area (acres): 761747.5 | 37.83N 119.50W

City/State Entered

Dates Visited

Weather

Temp

Where We Stayed

Who Was With Me

What We Did

Sights

Wildlife

Impressions

My Favorite Memory

I Visited

- ◯ Yosemite Valley
- ◯ Half Dome
- ◯ Yosemite Falls
- ◯ Glacier Point
- ◯ El Capitan
- ◯ Vernal Falls

- ◯ The Ahwahnee
- ◯ Bridalveil Fall
- ◯ Tunnel view
- ◯ ....
- ◯ ....
- ◯ ....

Next Time I Will

Notes

Will Return?

Yes / No

Overall Experience

Zion

Utah | EST. 1919 | Area (acres): 147242.66 | 37.30N 113.05W

City/State Entered

Dates Visited

Weather

Temp

Where We Stayed

Who Was With Me

What We Did

Sights

Wildlife

Impressions

My Favorite Memory

I Visited

- ○ The Narrows
- ○ Angels Landing
- ○ Emerald Pools Trail
- ○ Canyon Overlook Trail
- ○ Observation Point Trail
- ○ Mount Carmel Highway

- ○ West Rim Trail
- ○ Weeping Rock Trail
- ○ The Subway
- ○ ....
- ○ ....
- ○ ....

Next Time I Will

Notes

Will Return?

Yes / No

Overall Experience

Your feedback is what keeps us going.
Please feel free to leave us an honest review on our product page.

Made in the USA
Las Vegas, NV
11 December 2022